Abba's

Little Princess

How I Found My Crown

Through the Cross

Iuvina Basile

To Caroline

No matter what, always Remember,

"For great is your love, higher than
the heavens; your faithfullness
reaches to the skies". Psalm 108:4

Urina R. Basil

Abba's Little Princess

Abba's Little Princess© 2020 Iuvina Basile

Printed in the United States of America

Front Cover and interior formatting designed by Victoria Lynn Designs
www.victorialynndesigns.com

Front Cover Art by Elizabeth Schmaltz

Published by Anchored In Faith LLC
Address: Wolfeboro, NH, 03894
Email: anchoredinfaith.hebrews619@gmail.com
Website www.anchored-in-faith.com

Paperback: 978-0-578-78084-9
E-book: 978-0-578-78085-6

Dedication

To

Dr. Nancy Boylan Alford. My therapist, translator of my Amygdala and my rock of five years. I look forward to seeing you in Heaven when the time comes.

I would also like to give credit where credit is absolutely due:

To Shannon Polk-who was my first seed into the ministry tree.

To OG (Pastor Billy Hardwick) for answering the call to not ONLY share the Gospel but to make disciples of ALL nations, for his obedience to God and all his time and effort in discipling me (MAJOR shoutout to his beautiful wife Heather Hardwick for putting up with us during bible studies, and for giving me her Bible, what a precious gift).

To Leslie Harder who God used to comfort me and pray with/for me in times of fear, pain and rebellion.

To Caroline Long and Susan Britt Maron 2 prayer warriors from God sent to intercede during desperate times.

To my 3 A's, A'la Jones, Andrea Ouellette and April Tribe Giauque, whom God sent for guidance, support, accountability and so much more.

And finally, to Chet, whom God brought into my life for such a powerful purpose. To help me grow in my calling and to help this book become a reality.

Abba's Little Princess

Abba's Little Princess

Introduction

When I first began to tell people about the book title Abba's Little Princess, most assumed it was a children's book. Hearing the words *Little Princess*, I can understand how that assumption can be made. When I would reply with, "no, it's not a children's book but geared to young ladies and women," I would get an "oh" back.

This book was and is designed to be read by countless young ladies struggling with their appearances, fitting in, with all the emotional chaos that comes with that season of their lives. This book was and is also designed to be read by women, whose past traumas have planted seeds of insecurities that grew into roots and strongholds, keeping them from fully walking into their God-given purpose and identities.

This book is written for the daughters of the King. Daughters who feel less than at times, who feel discouraged in who they are and who have allowed insecurities to distort the reflection staring back at them in the mirror. Each page is sealed with some aspect of darkness in the form of pain, hopelessness, trauma, and then with the light of Jesus, which brings on love, grace, and hope.

It is a journey that I pray you will willingly take, not only because I want you to, but because you know in your heart, deep down into your spirit that *something is missing*; *it's just not right.* You are tired of asking the question, "how much longer can I go on feeling like this?"

I am here to tell you that if you choose to commit to yourself, your faith walk to the One who knitted you together in your mother's womb, your life will be forever changed. Are you willing to open your heart and your mind and expose your chains of insecurities and walk with me and our Savior into freedom? If you said "Yes" then I ask you to continue reading until the very last page.

Abba's Little Princess

Table of Contents:

Abba's Little Princess

CHAPTER 1

My Prison

Prison is a cold, dark, lonely, and dangerous place. The main purpose is punishment. It is a consequence to somebody's actions. However, that is only physically describing prison. What about when someone is emotionally and mentally imprisoned? Is that even a thing? Well my beloved, I'm here to tell you it is. Being incarcerated by your own mind, bound with the feelings of emotional imprisonment of the lies of the enemy and enslaved by the consequences of the actions of self and others is a very real thing.

I always say you don't have to be in a physical prison building in order to be locked up. If it's okay, my lovely's, I would like to open my cell door and let you into my prison, where the walls were constructed not by cement or brick but by the words of my family. The warden is not a middle-aged man, but the very entity that was kicked out of heaven.

As a warning, I do have one suggestion before you walk into the gates of my insecurities. Look for the similarities and not the differences. Sometimes it is about the emotional bondage shared and the state of mind versus identical experiences. Now that you have made it through the gates of my prison, let the journey begin.

In the real world, there are different types of prisons, however their purpose is the same. All tangible prisons have cells that make up each housing unit. Each cell has a steel door (some have bars), three walls and a ceiling. It looks like a gloomy and hopeless box. All prisons have actual names, mine is called *Insecurities Maximum*

Facility. Maximum prisons usually house the most dangerous of all the inmates. And trust me when I say there is danger when you are walking around in chains of the baggage of your childhood trauma.

I have been living in my cell of *not good enough* since I can remember. My first wall in my cell is made up of the insecurity of my weight. A very popular issue among women, and sure, some people would just say get over it. But is that the answer? What about, "just eat healthy and exercise." Sometimes the answer is not that simple and just like concrete walls in a prison, it is not easy to break through. Part of my overweight journey deals with health issues and medications. It's not always about grilled chicken salads and gym memberships.

In fact, I've had a gym membership off and on since I was five years old, yes you read correctly five. When I was about five years old, I lost two teeth around the same time. So, like all children, I was super excited to put them under my pillow. In my culture the tooth fairy works first-shift so a tooth or teeth in my case are placed

3

under the pillow before school so when I came back from school, my gifts would be under my pillow (Our tooth fairy gave gifts not money). When I came back that afternoon, I saw my pillows were moved and I shook with excitement. My mind racing with thoughts of a new stuffed animal or a new doll.

I ran up to my bed and moved my pillow to unveil this wonderful surprise only to be met with emotions I could no quiet put my five-year-old fingers on. Have you ever seen something, and you get that uneasy "this is wrong" feeling? A moment where it felt like time stood still because you were trying to take in the event and make sense of it?

That was me, in that moment, my excitement faded and waves of hurt began to flood my body. Under the pillows were two of the ugliest track suits, I've ever seen. One was a dark plumb purple, and it had the Simpson's on it. There loca a pack of socks next to a pair of new white balance tennis shoes. Next to the Tennis shoes is what made my little heart drop. It was a

4

paper ID card; in reality it was my gym membership. I was only five years old. I remember my mom standing at the door and she softly said, "Now you can become beautiful." Was I not beautiful? What was so wrong with me at five that the tooth fairy felt I deserved a gym membership and exercise gear instead of a stuffed animal?

Unfortunately, all the exercise in the world would not eradicate my weight issues because part of it is my health diagnosis, which was not given to me until many, many, years later as an adult. You see, there are three parts to my weight wall in my prison:

1) The physical (my health challenges)

2) Mental (how I look at myself) and

3) Emotional (how I feel about my body).

There is a psychological component to being a prisoner of your own mind. Cycles start to develop, and I am no different. The major cycle I go through would start when I lose weight and the feeling it would bring, but then I would gain some of it back. With the weight I would gain back I made sure to bring a bucket of insults to beat myself up with and then get depressed; just to lose weight again to feel happy and the cycle would start all over again.

Physically, an inmate feels trapped by the consequences of their actions and choices. Mine is the entrapment of my childhood trauma (and not everything I experienced is highlighted in this book). Comments from family members asking me why I was still fat when they would see me ring in my ears like the slamming of the metal doors when a cell closes. My weight is attached to much more than just a number on a scale. Its filled with rude comments by bullies, its linked to starving myself in military school all wrapped up in my Sicilian culture where murder can be justified but being overweight cannot.

Let's be honest, America's view on beauty was also a standard I would never reach. It didn't matter that my family would control my food when I was younger. The more I grew in age, the more I grew in width. I remember one night at dinner, my mom made my favorite, Sheppard's, pie. I can smell the aroma of buttered mash potatoes and seasoned ground beef even now as I'm writing. She grabbed my plate and placed three tablespoons of it on my plate. I looked in excitement as surely more was coming but it never did. she walked away to put the pot back on the stove.

"Mom is this all? "I asked,

"Yes." She said.

"Why?" I asked.

"Do you think You NEED more?" She said. I looked at my parents' plates and they had at the very least double the portion, I had.

I replied, "I'm hungry." My dad looked at me and said, "Then eat. Why are you always obsessing over food?"

I had no idea that wanting more than a couple of tablespoons constituted as being obsessive over food. I would feel so alone and so worthless in those moments. I can clearly remember thinking, *there must be something wrong with me, if I want more food.* It turns out I was just hungry.

As the years went on, my issues went with me. No matter how many times an inmate gets transferred, they always end up back in a cell with those horrible concrete walls. Mine were engraved with the mentality that only thin girls were beautiful, popular, and loved. And because I was none of those ideas, I didn't deserve any of those wonderful things. I remember using humor as a defense mechanism early on. I would think to myself, "if I make the bullies laugh then maybe, just maybe, they'll forget the next punch line that makes others laugh at me and my body."

One of the memories that still makes me cringe is about the school desk. You know the desk in which I am referring to: the table armchair with the tiny plastic chair attached to it. Also known as a *torture device*. I can still feel my heartbeat pounding in my ears as the memories of my feet walking towards that imprisonment device right before class started to flood my mind.

Dread and hesitation rose up inside as I got closer to the place where I would have to wrestle and twist like a pig in gridle. I tried to bend and slip to the side without sticking my fanny in the next row. "Ugh, disgusting!" I hear from the student behind me who now can't even see the board because Shamu just attempted to fit and sit down in this tiny desk made for *normal* people.

I take a long deep breath once I finally sat down, partially because I needed my stomach to shrink and partially because squeezing into the plastic and metal device is exhausting. As I sigh, I hear "mooing" from behind me. My head just falls down in a sigh of just sadness mixed with wishful thinking of how I wish I wasn't here in this classroom with these students, in this small desk.

Don't get me wrong, I am a nerd at heart, and I love learning but the abuse that comes with being physically present in class just doesn't seem worth it. I'm thinking "if I just look down for this next hour, I will be okay. "Iuvina, will you pass out the graded assignments to the class, please?" I hear the teacher say. She cannot be freaking serious right now.

I feel the side of my body already sticking to my fat Rolls. *NO, NO, absolutely not.* I think to myself. *Someone else can do it, why does it have to be me?* But instead I say, "yes ma'am," and I push with my arms, praying to the Greek Gods as I try to slip around. *Suck it in*, I think to myself, but instead I hear the scrapping of the desk legs against the linoleum floor. *Someone please kill me!* I scream internally as I bring the desk with me.

All I can hear is explosive laughter echoing around the classroom as the other students point and laugh at the hippo that is me, a freak show if you will. As I finally pop from the desk and walk to the front of the room, I look at my teacher in the eyes. I know she sees mine filled with tears. I pass the papers out then ask her if I can go to the bathroom. She nods yes and I walk out of the classroom leaving the laughter and mooing behind me.

Inmates feel trapped all day long, and I felt no different as I was trapped in my own body without escape. I always felt that people assumed all I ever did was sit on my butt and eat all day and night. If they only knew the truth of how I have always been active and loved the outdoors, how fresh fruit was my favorite. That even when my parents controlled my sugar intake and we only ate fried food once a month, nothing made the difference.

As I grew older my trauma of being bullied and having my food controlled, led to a very twisted relationship between me and food and essentially the way I felt about myself and my body. I began to not really feel comfortable eating in public because of people starring and judging me (and maybe they weren't but that's how I felt). I was comfortable with my inner circle which was only a couple of friends but that's it, and definitely not around guys. I would drop my fork in a heartbeat and push my plate away from me, I felt guilty for eating more than a couple of bites. I remember going on a casual date one time with a guy, we went to a taco place and he told me to go ahead and order.

"One taco and a small drink, please?" I whispered. We got our food, sat down, and started talking. Before we left, he asked me if I had enough to eat since half my taco was still on my food tray. "Oh yes I'm stuffed," I lied. I hadn't eaten anything else that day but obviously the guy was just being nice. No way he would take me out again or even look at me if I sat down and ate two whole tacos.

As life went on it involved more turmoil with food and relationships until one year, I got pregnant and then married (a bit backwards I know). Everything started to change a few years after I had my son. I started to experience such strong sugar and carb cravings throughout the month that I would go into eating binges (always in the privacy of my own home of course). I would be sitting at home watching tv and I would look down only to see an empty foot-long sandwich wrapper, a demolished peanut M&M's party bag (the one-pound bag) and a small ice cream container that only contained a spoon in it.

I remember walking passed my room to the bathroom and caught a glimpse of myself in the mirror. I looked at my chunky face, my round stomach trying to bust out of my sweatpants, and I thought to myself *you ugly repulsive excuse for a woman*! *This is why nobody will ever truly love You. This is why your relationships don't last. This is why your parents hate you. Look at you! Disgusting!*

That pattern and the self-bullying continued; And by the years of 2014-2015 I reached my heaviest weighing in at 235 pounds, more than I weighed when I was 9 months pregnant. Not only was I physically heavy but I was also overcome with shame, depression, anxiety, and self-hate. No longer were classmates mooing and my parents making daily bullying comments. This time the degradation was coming from the reflection starring back at me.

That is how my first prison wall was built—a wall entirely based on my weight. The second wall brings more shame and embarrassment and isolation. It is the very reason why I told God *no* the first time he told me to write this book. An entire year and a half running away from my God given mission just so I would not have to expose this part of my *imprisonment*. My second wall is not made out of concrete but more like hair; facial hair to be exact.

You know, one of the most distinct physical features that separates men from women. After all women are *not supposed* to have beards, mustaches, and sideburns, right? I am not supposed to look like I howl at a full moon, right? And yet, here I am in all my hairy glory unless I wax or shave and pretend, I don't battle with this deep dark fuzzy secret. I'm not talking about peach fuzz or a few chin hairs. No, what I'm talking about is teenage-boy-returning-to-8th-grade-the-summer-after-he-hit-puberty kind of hair. I can blame it on being diagnose with PCOS (Polycystic ovary syndrome) at age 14, yet since my hysterectomy in 2015, my hormone levels have been fine. I can blame it on being Sicilian, after all people from those parts tend to have more hair on them.

I can come up with tons of justifiable reasons why I was given a fuzzy face and yet none of them ever made me feel less insecure about myself. In fact, even more so than my weight, my facial hair has been my number insecurity since freshman year of high school. My 9th grade year, sitting in honors world history (still stuck in that stupid tiny desk), I was scratching under my chin when I felt a few hairs. I was a bit confused, didn't think women could get facial hair but I let it go and focused on the teacher instead. when I went home that day, I looked in the mirror and there under my chin were several strands of hair. I'm was a 15-year-old girl, who was growing a beard!

The horror that I felt was indescribable. My heart sank down to my large stomach and I started to panic. So, I did the only thing I knew guys did with facial hair and grabbed a razor and shaving cream and shaved off those hairs. In my head I thought "problem solved" and went about my business. A few days later as I am looking in the mirror before school, I notice black specs under my chin, I look closer and in pure terror I realized those specks were tiny hairs.

Not only were the hairs growing back but there was more this time. I hear my dad yelling" hurry up or you will miss the bus". Is he serious? I can't go to school like this. What am I going to do?! I can't tell my dad "sorry dad can't go to school because I'm growing a beard!" I take a deep breath and try not to cry as I headed out of the apartment and off to school. I spent that entire school day with my head down as my long curly hair acted as curtains to my face. And yet deep down I just knew people were starring, that somehow people knew about my new secret and were just waiting for the right time to yell out" here comes the bearded lady".

As time went by, I shaved more and more watching the color of those hairs go from brown to black and the texture going from soft to rough. I continued to keep my head down when I walked. I still used my actual hair to cover my face. I can't put my finger on the exact date my mustache decided to make an appearance, but it did. It's like I woke up one morning and looked in the mirror and there it was, joining the facial hair party. I knew at that moment that whatever ounce of self-esteem might have been hiding deep in me was about to be shaved off right along with my fuzzy face.

As if high school and being a plump teenage girl, isn't hard enough, my face was now growing a full beard with hair under my chin, on my cheeks and now my upper lip. I remember one day when I was walking home with my best friend and out of nowhere, he points out that I was growing sideburns. He used the words "you are as hairy as a werewolf." I stopped walking, from the embarrassment and pain as he had so coldly pointed *that* out to me with obvious no regards to my feelings. I remember getting home, going into my room and laying on my bed while the tears began to fall. *Who is going to want to be friends let alone date a hairy fat girl?* I said to myself. *I just know I'm going to be alone forever.*

As I grew older and started to date, I was extremely cautious about guys touching my face. Even when one of my boyfriends tried to be romantic and grab my face to kiss me, I freaked out and yelled at him for touching my face. They didn't understand, but my scars caused by my insecurities were very real to me. Looking in the mirror quickly became my least favorite thing to do. All it did was shed light to my hairs on my face and re-confirmed that no matter what I wore I still looked like a cow with clothes on.

The self-hate speech continued, the *I'm not worthy of love* mindset carried on. That deep hateful voice that always reminded me that I will forever be alone still spoke until a faithful New Year's Eve night. I remember parts of that night. I was at a party with all my friends. I remembered being given the infamous Red Solo cup. I didn't ask what was in it, I just began to drink. The strong and sour taste was mixed with a hint of strawberries. I handed the now empty cup back and another one was given, I quickly finished that one and as I waited for my third cup something wonderful happen, I began to feel warm all over, my thoughts began to slow down and that voice that spews hate was silenced. I remember feeling good for the first time in my life.

Unfortunately, that was also the night that the door was blown wide open for my addiction to take over my life and me. After that night I started to drink at every party and not just drinking socially, I mean drinking until I passed out.

Later on in my life this would lead to other drugs. I did not want to lose that *good feeling* when I would get high and drunk, I was no longer the fat girl with facial hair that nobody cared about. I was the fun, loving, life of the party that people loved to hang out with. You see most of us (addicts) use drugs to not feel that pain that we carry. Anytime I was using. my insecurities melted away however what was really happening is I was being enslaved by addiction.

My third and final prison wall was not necessary built on in securities but by the disease of Addiction. I would spend the next almost ten years being yanked by the chain of needing to use by any means while my life and body were being destroyed. Even though my insecurities, and self-hatred was not the only pain I was numbing by using it was a very big part of it. I would give up anything for that feeling and eventually I did just that, I went from an overweight bearded lady to a Junkie on the street.

I won't ever forget the night I met some friends at a bar after work. It was 20 minutes until last call, so I had to make that short time count. I quickly devoured 12 shots of vodka in that timeframe. The room began to spin, and the bar conversations became distant muffles. I knew my friends were leaving so I tried to stand, and man was that a bad idea. I held to every table and chair as I waddled to the front door. Right as I got by the door the weight of my legs got to be too much and I fell down. Instead of getting back up I started to crawl.

I crawled out of the bar right into a snow filled parking lot. I remember the throbbing pain of my hands as I crawled in the snow. Feeling wet patches all over my body because my clothes were getting soaked by the snow as I dragged myself right into the next bar next door. The next morning, I woke up in my bed with no memory of the second bar I crawled into or how I made it home.

———————————

One of the most popular statements offenders make is *I don't know how I got here*. This refers to the feeling of overwhelming pain mixed in with consequences of their actions.

I remember asking myself this very question one night, while I was homeless. I began to say out loud to God (whom I knew existed but had no clue who He was or what He was really about) *what am I missing? How did I get here? Why can't I live like others do?* Suddenly it was like a movie began to play and God showed me my addiction and that in fact I am an addict and it's not too late to get help.

That was the beginning of my recovery journey. That night was a *spiritual awakening* as we call it in the rooms of recovery. I will never forget it and I am so grateful for it because without being clean and in recovery I would have never gotten the chance to be saved, get baptized and discipled. Without those steps I would have never gotten to know God, the one true living God, and how much He genuinely loves this chubby addict with facial hair.

CHAPTER 2

Gods Point of View

Do you remember that phrase WWJD (what would Jesus do)? It was almost a national movement with youth ministries making plastic bracelets with those letters printed to give away to all the kids. As if when we needed help or advice, we would automatically think about *what would Jesus do*, and suddenly that wisdom would come to us, and we would magically act like Jesus. Do not get me wrong, I love that statement, and I do think it's vital that we think and act like Christ. However, that wisdom does not magically enter our minds by wearing a plastic bracelet. That wisdom is

24

found in our relationship with God via prayer, fasting, and reading and applying His word.

In thinking about WWJD, I began to realize that I never asked myself an important question during this journey. How does Jesus feel? What is God's perspective on my insecurities? Self-bullying? The answer? I never even thought about it. And if you also said, "no, I don't think about God's point of view often" do not worry; you are not alone in this. I had no earthly idea how He felt about women with facial hair. Not once did I ever stop and think WW G P V (what was God's point of view) on me and my insecurities.

Now part of that, I can blame it on not being saved, but can I actually? And the rest I can blame it on? Well, let's get real. There is no justification for why I placed God's word on the back burner **especially** after I was saved. The good news is, that it is a new day, and with that comes a fresh start. The thing about thinking about God's perspective is that we need to know His word first.

To understand His point of view, we must know where it's coming from. For example, my friends know my stance on abortion without me having to express my opinion on it. How? Because they know me. So, to get God's point of view on all of this, I (we) must know God. I will say this when getting to know God, go to the source. When someone has a question about or for me, I prefer they come to me personally instead of going to question my friends. Now that's not to Say God can't send you mentors because He can. I have personally found it best to go directly to God, and when ready, He will send you a trusted servant.

What did I need to know about God to get to know His point of view on insecurities, self-hate, body shaming? I think a great place to start is by asking two simple questions: what are we to God? and how does He truly feel about us? Once I knew the answers to these two questions, then I was able to see God's actual perspective on this matter.

What are we to God? When I first asked myself, what am I to Him, I felt almost silly asking, but then I realized that specifically, I had no idea. Was I a little ant that He looked down upon when He was bored? Was I something that got on His nerves a lot, as I did with my earthly parents? How do I find these answers? Well, just like I previously said, His word. His word shines light to my dark moments. It also points to answers when I have questions.

What am I to God? I am His child. That is a title that quickly became one of my favorites that God gave me. Galatians 3:26 says, "so in Christ Jesus, you are all children of God through faith." I do not know about you, but I am super excited to have God as my Heavenly Father! The perfect Creator, the King of Kings and Lords of Lord's, is my daddy. Now, that is something to boast about! Of course, it does not stop there, because He always gives more. What am I to God? His incredible masterpiece.

Ephesians 2:10 says, "For we are God's handiwork, created in Christ Jesus to do good works, which God prepared in advance for us to do." Another translation says workmanship instead of handiwork. Furthermore, in Genesis 1:26 and 28, we are His creation. Wow, I am so much to God, and yet so little to myself. I can only assume that God was utterly heartbroken when I would bully myself every time I looked in the mirror, how I looked straight as His child, His creation, His design, and called it ugly, disgusting, unworthy, not enough, and unloved.

The example God gave me in understanding this topic was this: picture your child, you can see both physical and personality traits that he/she received from you. One day you are walking down the corridor of your home. Out of the corner of your eye, you see your child looking at themselves in the mirror. You just stand there and smile at them and think what a beautiful gift from God. And then you hear them say "ugh I hate myself, look at this red hair, I look so stupid! These clothes are so ugly; no one will ever like me looking like this." How would you feel?

Your beautiful and wonderful child that is not only your child to you, but a gift, heart of hearts and a blessing, just called themselves ugly and ugly because of things you gave them such as the red hair that you also have and the brand new clothes you just bought them for school, AND they hate themselves. If you are a parent like me, I would be devastated. I would probably cry and even feel some anger. Also, if you do not have kids, think about how you would feel if your niece or nephew felt this way.

When I use hate speech against myself, I am not only speaking death over myself, over God's creation, but I am also speaking it against God. Me operating on insecurities and body shaming is me rejecting God's child. Therefore, I am rejecting Him because in Genesis 1, both verses 26 and 28 states, "I was created in His image."

So then, the next question now that I know I am so many beautiful and amazing things to God is, how does God truly feel about us? Does He like us a lot, does He love us? What are His feelings? One of the world's most famous verses comes to mind immediately when I thought about this question. John 3:16, "For God so LOVED the world that He gave His one and only son, that whoever believes in Him shall not perish but have eternal life." I didn't have to go very far into this verse to read and realize how He truly feels about not just me, but us.

We, you and I and the rest of the entire world are loved! Simply and yet so powerfully said. He loves us so much that He made the ultimate sacrifice, sent His one and only son to the cross. God so loves the fat, ugly, fuzzy faced, an ashamed and worthless feeling girl that would stare back at me when I passed by a mirror that Christ Jesus was crucified so I could be saved and have eternal life with the creator (Excuse me while I burst into tears).

Have you ever heard or seen the movie *The Passion of the Christ*? The movie title itself gives it away, passion meaning strong, amorous feeling or desire, love. The title indicates the love of Christ. If you have not yet seen this movie, I highly suggest that you do and bring tissues (like lots of them) because you are going to need it. It's a movie that walks you through the final moments of Jesus before and then during His crucifixion. I will warn you; it is a bit graphic; however, watch it anyways.

I remember watching this movie for the very first time in military school, a year after it was released. I was sixteen years old; I was in a large room with about 80 other cadets. We sat in rows, very close to each other, basically packed like a can of sardines. We were not told beforehand the movie that we were going to see. Instead, the lights were dimmed, and the film began to play.

The room was quiet, until a quarter of the ways through this movie, it wasn't anymore. All you could hear is sniffling, crying, and noise of shock. I was one of those people making those noises. To this day, I cannot watch *The Passion of The Christ* without sobbing. I'm crying now just thinking about it. To make the connection that every moment I looked in the mirror, hating on myself, must have felt to God, how every single one of those lashes felt to Jesus. It's just a different point of view because it's not my own but His.

Romans 5:8 state's "But God demonstrates His own love for us in this: while we were still sinners, Christ died for us." If that doesn't make a statement of how He truly feels about us, how greatly He loves me, then I don't know what can. Do you know how many times the word love is written in the bible? A whole bunch (that's my numeric system). Let's look at 1 John 4:16 "God is love. Whoever lives in love lives in God, and God in them." God loves me and God, loves you too. One of my favorite verses ever, we love because He first loved us (1 John 4:19) has been forever engraved in my heart. I am capable of love because He first loved me. WOW!

One of my favorite things about God (and there are many) is that He is never changing and everlasting. He doesn't love me one day, and then here I go messing up, and He changes His mind. He is eternal and never changing; He is who He has always been and will always be. He doesn't toss His love for us aside like an out of style outfit. His love is NEVER out of style.

In Deuteronomy 10:17, this is confirmed to us "For the Lord, your God is God of gods and Lord of lords, the great God, mighty and awesome, who shows no partiality and accepts no bribes." You can't even pay God not to be who He is. So how does God truly and honestly feel about us? He loves us so much that neither fear, death, bribery, or any sin can stop His love for us.

Paul said it best in Romans 8:38-39 "For I am convinced that neither death, nor life, neither angels or demons, neither the present nor the future, nor any powers, neither height nor depth, nor anything else in all creation, will be able to separate US from the LOVE of God that is in Christ Jesus our Lord." Paul said convinced (or persuaded in the KJV), which means utterly certain about something.

I am His creation, His workmanship, His handiwork, His child whom He loves more than all creations. It is written in the bible, the Holy word of God, "and how more valuable you are than a bird?" Luke 12:24.

God never made me to call myself ugly or grow up insecure. It doesn't say, so God created mankind in His image but then realized He made a mistake. What happened was the creator created His creation out of perfect self-Image and inspiration. How many times have I called myself *fat and ugly* and proclaimed to be *unloved* because of my *facial hair and weight*? Too many times to count really, and yet God never called me those things. Ephesians 2:10 never said, "for I am fat and fuzzy (insert your insecurities here) created to self-hate because God didn't know what He was doing when He made me, so I have to walk in self-doubt and shame forever."

I connect this with the time I picked out a gift for my son. It wasn't a holiday, or anything just wanted to show him how much I loved him and how much he means to me. I remember him talking about a game. So, I worked hard, saved up, looked all over the place, and finally bought him the game. The day I planned on giving it to him, I was bursting with excitement. I wrapped it up in some awesome Star Wars gifting paper (my son was named after a character from that franchise), and I waited impatiently for him to come home from school.

As soon as he walked into the house, I shouted, "I have a surprise for you!". He started to get excited and could not wait, so I handed him the badly wrapped gift (gift wrapping is not a talent God gave me). I watched him aggressively tear the paper away so he could get to what was inside. And then, I watched his reaction. Instead of the twinkle in his eyes, I received the "I can't believe this is it" expression followed by "Mom you got the wrong game!" and he stomps away while I am left in the kitchen alone and devasted.

Is this what God feels every time I say *I am not good enough, I am not worthy of love, I am disgusting, I am horrible looking and so forth and so on?* Am I telling

God, I can't believe this is me? I can't believe this is what you picked out for me? How many times have I basically said, "Obviously, Lord, you made a mistake!"

What is something valuable to you? Maybe you just bought a brand-new car? Maybe you're the first one in your family to graduate college and so you have your degree mounted in a pretty frame. So, what if your vehicle gets wrecked or the frame breaks and rips your degree? How would you feel? Now, what if your child or someone you cherish more than a car or degree gets hurt? How Would You Feel then? Especially when they are the ones causing the hurt to themselves.

Now how much more grief does our Abba feel when we damage ourselves with words that pierce all the goodness, He has created in us. Let's stay in that moment for a little longer, close your eyes, and feel...What did you feel? Hurt? Sadness? Shock? Mourning? Even a bit of anger? Those are all the things I felt, too, and some days still do.

Another aspect of my downward spiral that I never thought about God's view on was the physical abuse I put myself through with my addiction. I was putting substances in my body that, at the very least, were unhealthy and, at the very worst, would kill me. I abused my body with what addiction put me through. I never cared about God's opinion on it because it was my body, my life, and who cares what others think, right? And yet this twisted mentality could not be furthest from the truth.

Paul says in 1 Corinthians 6:19, "Or do you not know that your body is a temple of the Holy Spirit within you, whom you have from God? You are not your own." Here I was destroying God's temple with all kinds of horrible things, not even caring. I never realized in a way that I do now that I belonged to the Lord almighty or that my body was the dwelling place of such a powerful and amazing God-given gift called the Holy Spirit.

37

It seemed that all the negative thoughts, all the self-bullying, all the ugly feelings I felt go directly against what God feels and considers me to be. So, since I now know without a shadow of a doubt, I am God's creation, a work of art, and He loves me more than I can ever fully comprehend, then why are insecurities a real thing? Why is this felt by so many? The insecure feelings are obviously not from God, so where do they come from?

CHAPTER 3

Spiritual Warfare

There is a war waging between death and life, good and evil, God and satan (yes the s is a lowercase s for a reason). And to think that before his fall, the devil was an angel and highly thought of according to Ezekiel 28:11-15. However, he fell, and with that, his name changed as well from Lucifer (morning star) (Isaiah 14:12) to what we call him today satan, which means adversary because that is what he is. He is our enemy because he is an adversary to God. He twists God's words to create doubt and tries to mimic everything God says.

God spoke, and creation happened, while satan likes to speak lies, change perception, and push sin to occur. If satan can keep convincing us to speak death over us (I'm not good enough, not loved, I don't matter, etc.), then he gets what he is after. The devil knows he can't win the war that has already been won and sealed by God almighty. What satan wants is to take as many down with him as possible with the time he has left. Will that be you?

I almost picture satan talking to God like he did in the book of Job. And satan saying something like "you see how your creation sees themselves? You created something that hates itself instead of praising you, hahaha." After all, the devil is a bully and enjoys shoving things in God's face. Anything to make it seem, less than who and what God truly is, the enemy is there for it!

Since there is a war going on, then warfare is taking place. Warfare is defined as the engagement in or the activities involved in war or conflict; because all of this is taking place in the spiritual, then we as believers refer it to spiritual warfare. The easiest way I like to explain it is, the enemy's activities or stunts to get us to fall just like he did.

Now some of you may be thinking okay, thanks for sharing your insecurities. I realize I have some of my own. Thanks for explaining the good versus evil thing, but what in the heck does that have to do with God and my faith and spiritual warfare? Well, I am glad you asked (even if you didn't ask). Let's unveil this first most straightforwardly before we dig deep in the word of God. Regardless of where you are in your faith walk, we can all say with confidence; God is real, and so is the devil. We all know that the enemy's task is to kill, steal, and destroy, and he has many ways of accomplishing that.

One of the easiest ways to derail someone is to make them think untrue things. So, let's say you are on a road trip, and you are following the GPS. Every turn it asks you to take is leading you to the right destination. But what if the GPS has the wrong address? Then that means you are being led to the wrong place, and that has consequences.

What if you were on a time crunch? What if you only had a set amount of gas money budgeted this trip? Now, you are at the wrong place, with wasted resources. What if the incorrect address were set by a jealous co-worker who didn't want you to arrive at the critical business meeting that could launch you into a promotion? Not only have funds been wasted, but now your purpose could potentially be jeopardized.

That, my friends, is precisely why the enemy uses your insecurities to further his agenda and try to de-rail you off your purpose and off of living your life the way God intended, in abundance. He has used this trick from the very beginning starting with Adam and Eve.

Let's take it back to the beginning, so to speak into the garden of Eden. After God created Adam, he told Adam in Genesis 2 verses 16 and 17 "And the Lord God COMMANDED the man, you are free to eat from any tree in the garden; but you MUST not eat from the tree of the knowledge of good and evil, for when you eat from it, you will certainly die." Those were the words spoken by God (remember that as we go further).

In Genesis 2 verse 25, after God created a woman from man, it said, "Adam and his wife were both naked, and they felt no shame." Wow! After being made the way they were created, both men and women didn't feel negative about themselves or their appearance; this is very important to remember because now we are about to see the very first exchange of warfare.

In Genesis 3 verse 1 is where satan makes his appearance, and he is described as crafty.

The enemy says, "Did God say, you must not eat from any tree in the garden?" Right here, at this moment, he is trying to create doubt and confuse the woman.

That reminds me of a personal story. One day at work,

my boss told me I could go home early. She said to me, "Hey, you can go ahead and go home; there is not much left to do here." So, I happily gathered my things to head out. One of my co-workers (who didn't like me very much) asked me what I was doing. I told her, "the boss said I could go home early. I'm getting my things so I can leave."

She (with an attitude of course) replies with, "Did she say that?" I started to doubt the words that I had just heard a few minutes prior. I went back and asked my boss if she actually said I could leave.

When you can make someone doubt somebody's word, the door is then left open for perception and misinterpretation to walk right on through. The enemy knows this. Doubt and hopelessness are his two favorite weapons.

In Genesis 3 verses 2 and 3, we see the woman replying "we may eat fruit from the trees in the garden, but God did say, you must not eat fruit from the tree that is in the middle of the garden, and you must not touch it, or you will die." The woman knows what God said, and that's what she is standing on in this conversation; however, the enemy is crafty like the serpent in the bible. In verse 4, satan replies with, "you will not certainly die." There at that moment, he is undermining God and His word. God did say they would die if they ate from that particular tree, yet the tactic that the devil loves to use is layering doubt with a lie. God said yes, you would die; the enemy says no, you won't die. In verse 5, he tries to misrepresent God, as stated before, which creates, even more doubt and uncertainty.

As we all know, both take a bite from the fruit that came from that tree. Something compelling happens in the middle of verse 7, "Then the eyes of both of them were opened, and they realized they were naked; so they sewed fig leaves together and made coverings for themselves."

Wait a minute! They had been named and unashamed since Genesis 2 verse 25, so why did they react that way suddenly? Now they are so embarrassed about their appearances that they went and made coverings for their bodies.

When the enemy tricked them into eating from the tree that would expose them to evil, THEN their bodies became something negative. It wasn't until the serpent came into the picture that the creation started doubting God's word, disobeying it, and then experience ill feelings.

In verse 8, we see the guilt experienced with shame heaped on top because, at the end of that verse, it says, "and they HID from the Lord God among the trees of the garden." Not only did they cover up their bodies, but they hid from God himself. In verse 10, another ill-feeling gets introduced: fear. "He answered, I heard you in the garden, and I was afraid because I was naked, so I hid."

When God confronts Adam about these feelings (Genesis 3:11). The man does something that I did for a very long time, shifted the blame to someone else. In verse 12, Adam blames his wife for what had just happened (even though at the beginning of Genesis 2, God had put the man in charge).

In verse 13, the woman admits to God that "the serpent deceived me, and I ate." There it is. The enemy's purpose since the beginning is to deceive, why? Because if he can lead us astray, then he can lead us away from God. Adam proved it by falling for the trap and then immediately hiding from God. The rest of Genesis 3 outlines the consequences because, for every choice made, there is most definitely a consequence attached to it. How proud the enemy must have felt for setting up God's creation and introducing them to the bad and the ugly. On that day, the lines of war were drawn because nothing was ever the same for humankind.

As long as satan can convince you to put self on the throne of your life and move God out the way, satan will be your biggest fan because he knows he is leading you to failure and ultimate death. He is even more pleasured if he can convince you to worship him versus God, satan always encourages self-interest.

He convinced man and woman to not only do something God said not to, but he tricked them into believing that they should want to, which means putting themselves above what God wanted. I heard this saying years ago. I can't even remember who I first heard it from "The devil won't bother you if you are living wrong." I don't necessarily believe he won't bother you; I think it's the fact that he won't try to trip you up if you are already not living, walking, and worshipping God the way we are called to do.

When thinking about the enemy, I always view him as a hater, Debby downer, a miserable entity. As I was writing one day, this viewpoint came to mind. I had a "friend" in my middle school days who I at least thought was my friend. We would go to class together, hang out after school, she knew all my secrets, and I just thought we were the best of friends. Well turns out that when I wasn't hanging out with her, she was spreading lies and rumors about me; she told others about my secrets and did not have my best interest at heart at all.

At face value, that is the enemy, he will try to make you think he is your best friend but at the end he is not even remotely close. However, he is crafty and that is why we have the saying "I sold my soul to the devil" (that is my opinion anyway). Why would anybody (and many have) sell their soul to the devil, unless the devil manipulated them into thinking he had something they wanted, and to do that you have to be skilled in manipulation.

Remember the serpent was called *crafty,* which is why knowing who the real enemy is, and knowing what spiritual warfare is and how to fight against it, is so very important. The enemy, unlike the movies tried to make us believe, does not come in a cloud of smoke in your home with horns and a pitchfork. He comes in many ways, and he tailors his ways to fit the particular person.

For example, your insecurity might be a birthmark, while one of mine is my facial hair; to attack both of us, he can't use the same script. Now the let's call it "theology" behind it is the same, he uses lies, manipulation, our sin, anxiety, fear, disobedience to God, and a bunch more to attack us with. One of the things I tell the women that I disciple is this "when you pray out loud, especially for something and a short amount of time later, you get it, test it". Just because it comes doesn't mean it came from God.

Both God and satan can hear your out loud prayers, so you need to discern where that answer comes from. Often, the enemy comes when we are in a weakened state. For me, it may be at a time where I lack sleep, or a major change has come, or I'm not sure how to deal with something immediately, so I feel lost. He came that way with Jesus also as it is described in Matthew 4:1-11. This scripture is particularly important because it shows you how the enemy operates once more. Jesus was hungry, His physical body was deprived at that moment, and just like a cue in a musical, here comes the devil.

However, in that verse, he is not called that; he is called the Tempter.

In verse 3, the enemy says to Jesus, "**If** You are the Son of God, command that these stones become bread." Hit the PAUSE button right here, did you catch that strategy? One simple word, IF. *IF* is a conjunction that can mean "in case that." Why is this important? Because the enemy went after Jesus's Identity to plant the seed of doubt, much as he did in the garden. Did God say that? IF you are the Son of God, etc. He likes to plant these seeds of the doubt first because it attacks the word of God immediately. And if satan can slither you out of the word of God, then you are left without a firm foundation that will keep you during times of trouble and hardships.

However, because Jesus knew who He was and whose He was, He replied with this in verse 4 "Jesus answered, "It is written: 'Man shall not live on bread alone, but on every word that comes from the mouth of God.'" BAM! The word of what? God! The enemy tried to convince Jesus to doubt the word of God, and Jesus came back

51

WITH the word of God. Now digging deeper into that, the enemy doesn't stop there; this shows you the enemy isn't a once and done type of vermin.

In verse 6, the Tempter stepped up his game and said this "**IF** you are the Son of God," he said, "throw yourself down. For it is written: He will command his angels concerning you, and they will lift you in their hands so that you will not strike your foot against a stone." Hit the PAUSE button again, did you see what the enemy did here? Yes, he used IF again, still trying to create doubt in Christ's identity; however, he also used God's word (in the wrong context of course) against Jesus', meaning, even the devil knows scripture. Which then means, we also better know it because what did Jesus do in the following verse? Use more of God's word against the enemy.

In verse 7, Jesus answered him, "It is also written: 'Do not put the Lord your God to the test." So, what happened next? The devil came at Jesus one more time, and this time he tried a different tactic, remember when I mentioned people selling their souls to satan, and how he must have made them offer they can't refuse? Well, watch it unveil here in verse 8 and 9; "Again, the devil took Him to a very high mountain and showed Him all the kingdoms of the world and their splendor. 'All this I will give you,' he said, "if you will bow down and worship me." What would your answer have been? Well, Jesus had enough of the enemy's shenanigans and replied with "Away from me, satan! For it is written: 'Worship the Lord your God and serve Him only."

Anytime the enemy tried it, Jesus came back with more truth. He stood His ground by staying firm on the foundation of who He is (The son of God), knowing whose He is (God the Father), and speaking the truth (The Holy word of God). Now a beautiful thing happens after verse 10, "Then the devil left Him, and angels came and attended Him" (Verse 11). The enemy had been defeated because he left, AND God sent angels to attend to Jesus. This means that God is aware of when we are tempted, and He is aware of when we are in trouble, and even through a storm, He will attend to us.

53

He said He would never leave us nor forsake us (Deuteronomy 31:6 and Hebrews 13:5), and He proved it here in that verse. Do you see how everything is connected? The enemy goes after God's word when he attacks, and he plants seeds of first doubt, then he manipulates because if he can change your perception and feelings, then he can convince you of anything.

Did you notice how he kept attacking Jesus Identity?

What I am about to tell you, I don't think I have ever disclosed to a single human, however I am being led to share it here, with you. When I was a teenager, I must have been about 11 years old; I began to think that I should have been born a boy. Somehow the big man upstairs had messed up, and I was born into the wrong body.

Why would I think that? Well, I "felt" that way because I loved boys clothes and shoes versus girl clothes, I was not into makeup at all, I loved being outside and getting dirty, I had no interest in nail polish or girly things and I was attracted to girls instead of

54

boys (that is a testimony for another time). Those are all characteristics of a boy, right? As I grew, I preferred hot wheels over barbies. Those things that I liked helped me get to the conclusion that I was in the wrong body.

I never told anybody this and just kept it to myself, until several years later, those feelings just vanished, and my likes started to change. Why? Because the enemy won't keep sticking around if his tactics are not working, as we were shown in scripture. What would have happened to me if I were a teen in today's times, and I had told somebody? Would they have helped feed into my "feelings" and perceptions? Would they have started me on hormone therapy? Or Suggested transitioning? Part of my identity is that I am a female, I was born a female and God makes no mistakes.

The enemy loves to try to get us to obsess on our feelings versus being focused on righteousness because most people act with their feelings and not in God's word. It's a strategy that works; you only need to look around and see what is happening in today's world. It's even in marketing, how many commercials for products and services have you seen that made you feel a certain way? Our insecurities affect us emotionally, mentally, and physically and all that affects how we live and how we walk out our faith walk.

For example, when I felt hopeless in relationships due to my low self-esteem and self-image, then how in the world could I do my part in sharing the good news of the Gospel, which is what Jesus has commanded all of us to do in Mark 16:15. If I feel hopeless, how can I share hope? And that is exactly where the enemy wants and needs us to be, in that state of mind for as long as possible. If I feel unworthy of love because of my physical appearance, then how can I move in love and show others the perfect love of God? I couldn't, and you never want to force such a powerful massage out of yourself when you are not operating out of that because you run the risk of sounding fake or not being real, and we never want to do that.

The evil plan is, "the more I see you believing these lies, the more you won't be up to living in your purpose." It's a pretty clever plan if you think about it! IF we all understood and walked in the truth and power of whose we are. We will be able to learn who we truly are and when that happens, we start operating and walking in our calling and that my beautiful friends is something the enemy cannot afford for us to do; so he doesn't want that to happen which means he will do anything and everything in his power to stop us.

Another purpose for spiritual warfare is to cause division and ugliness, among others. God commanded us to love our neighbors as we love ourselves (Mark 12:31). Which means how can we love others if we do not first love ourselves? Hence why the enemy comes at us first, and then he uses our junk, so to speak to negatively impact others. Let me give you the example God put on my heart two years ago. Ever thought "that's a skinny girl problem" or "must be nice to have all that beautiful long hair?" What about "girl, I wish I could look like you?"

I am sure we have all thought these thoughts or similar or have even said them out loud to someone. I know I have said all three of them. After all, I have thick curly hair that looks like a bird's nest versus beautiful shiny straight hair. My body is shaped like a snake that ate something too big for its body (round is a shape, right?) Also, I wear glasses because I have a lazy eye; that's right. One of my eyes puts himself in time out. I'm just a hot mess (have you ever called yourself that?)

And yet at this very moment while I'm writing this one of my sister's in Christ is texting me, and the text says, "acknowledge what you have." How ironic that as I'm sitting here explaining what I wish I had, I get this message. I have often said and heard "must be nice to have that problem" (like really? Who the heck wishes they had problems?). I usually say it to someone who looks like how I wish I looked like or to someone who has the life I wish I had.

This is where I have chosen to embrace the lies of the enemy instead of being humble and acting like Christ.

How so? Because usually, when I say, "I wish I had your problems," it's in response to a friend needing to express their hurts, their feelings and just needed someone to talk to. Yet, instead of listening and offering support and taking this time to speak life into a friend, I'm ignoring THEIR moment. I'm moving a conversation that is supposed to be about them back on me (can we say selfish?). Instead of being here in the moment with them, I'm too busy telling them how their problems don't matter. Am I so messed up about how I feel and see myself that I can't even stop the self-hating and projecting to be there for someone else without making remarks?

The enemy has engulfed me with such insecurities, and I have accepted the lies to the point that I can't even fully be a good friend to someone. That is a hard pill to swallow; however, the truth is often hard to accept but necessary to move forward. How many times as women have we done this in conversations with our girlfriends? We can't have revelation without realization, so in this moment of truth, however delicate, it's necessary.

Body shaming is exactly that regardless of what the person looks like. Curly hair, straight hair, tall, short, skinny, plus size, etc. Why does this matter so much? We will stand in the church house and testify how God is the creator, He is good, how He is the potter, and we are the clay, and yet we sometimes act, think and speak about us and others like He made a mistake in making us this way when He sculpted us.

Psalms 139:14 says, "I praise you because I am fearfully and wonderfully made, your works are wonderful. I know that full well." We are His works, and we are to praise Him, yet there have been times where I couldn't apply or believe this verse because I believed the devil when he called me unworthy, and not enough. I chose to accept the illusion that society put together that looks, and only certain looks are attractive, that only those attributes matter, and only if you have those can you be successful; while God's word says otherwise.

Psalm 46:5 says, "God is within her she will not fall," it doesn't say morph your bodies so you can remain attractive in the public eye forever. The lies of the enemy sprinkled with the skewed definition of beauty that society marketed warped how I viewed myself, therefore, the view in the mirror has never been to my liking because it doesn't match up to those standards and definitions.

For so long, I wanted to fix what I was ashamed of and embarrassed about because of how I felt. I was made to believe I needed to fix something that was never broken. I wanted to turn myself into something completely different, trying to morph myself into a different standard of worth, beauty, love, and attraction when in fact, it's not my standards or societies that matter but God's. We did not create ourselves; God created us, so why wouldn't we take Him on His word?

I would never have thought that my insecurities and spiritual warfare were connected. Never in a million years, my solid human brain would have put those two things together, and yet they are very much connected. The enemy uses anything he can against us, so it makes perfect sense that he would use our identities. If people are not rooted in the Creator, then the have no idea not only of who they are but of their potential, and the enemy is banking on that.

If you never realize who and whose you are and all the benefits that come with that, then you will never live a full, abundant kingdom-minded life, which means less trouble for the enemy. In the process of self-discovery, according to the maker, you also get to know more about HIM. So, of course, the enemy wouldn't want you to know any of this. The enemy is banking on fear, anxiety, ignorance, and imprisonment all of the things insecurities bring because if you are in prison, then you can't be free to live the righteous life God has set for you, and that is a win for the enemy.

I will share one more testimony with you; I struggled with suicidal ideation since I was five years old (remember the tooth fairy story?). I was finally able to put a name to that feeling when I was seven years old. I remember standing in the hallway of my best friend's house, eavesdropping on my mother and her mother talking about me. My mother was telling my best friend's mom not to give me any food (during snack time and dinner) because I was fat.

The way my mom annunciated the word *fat*, sounded like nails on a chalkboard. It was right then that I was finally able to identify the feeling I so often felt, it was called suicidal. I no longer wanted to be alive. I was tired of being called fat and treated like a leper. I was tired of my food being controlled, the anxiety of shopping for clothes since most would never fit, and I was especially tired of my mother telling other people not to feed me.

Since I am so horrendous, then why am I alive? I no longer wanted to be. I wanted out, out of the house, out of my family, out of this world. I carried those feelings for most of my life until I finally tried it. I have attempted suicide more times than I can count, from drowning myself, to speeding and trying to crash my car, and finally from overdosing (that attempt actually took my life, and by the grace of God it was restored).

The enemy was banking on me dying; however, God had a purpose. Why would the enemy want me dead? Because if I were killed and buried, then several people would not have come to Christ. I would not have been a disciple to a dozen women. My son would have never gotten to witness my salvation and baptism, which encouraged his journey with God. He felt the love in his heart grow, and he also was saved and baptized. The stories of love and life continue. Your life is a vital part of the bigger plan. Never forget that!

Don't let the enemy win, "stay alert! Watch out for your great enemy, the devil" (1 Peter 5:8a), don't be a casualty in spiritual warfare. The good news is that we have victory.

Are you ready to walk in the victory that we have through Christ Jesus?

CHAPTER 4

Victory

In 1 Corinthians chapter 15, verse 57 it says, "But thanks be to God! He gives us the victory through our Lord Jesus Christ." This verse talks about overcoming death (sin) through our savior who died on the cross for us. We have victory because Jesus conquered sin and death. This was especially important for me to learn as I battled my insecurities and allowed them to be the ruler of my life. The turnaround point for me was about (and this is a rough estimate) two years after I was saved.

Once I began to dig deep down into God's word and learned how God felt about me, how He viewed me, and that His word always rains true no matter what it looks like in the world. If I am to bear that name, that title of CHRISTIAN, then I must know, accept, and obey the word of God No matter what I think or what the world says.

The book of James is one of my favorites, like the entire book. James chapter 1 verses 22-25 clearly tells us, believers, what we are supposed to do with God's word.

22 Do not merely listen to the word, and so deceive yourselves. Do what it says. 23 Anyone who listens to the word but does not do what it says is like someone who looks at his face in a mirror 24 and, after looking at himself, goes away and immediately forgets what he looks like. 25 But whoever looks intently into the perfect law that gives freedom and continues in

it—not forgetting what they have heard but doing it—they will be blessed in what they do.

Jesus breaks chains, including those that shackle us in insecurities, self-hate, body shaming, embarrassment, shame, anxiety, depression, and all other cords attached to how we view ourselves and even others.

The word of God is enormously important to me, and so is sharing the Gospel and making disciples. It is a mission I take very seriously, and I have a passion for teaching women about God, how He views them, and how to deepen their relationship with Him. However, none of this would have been possible if God had not saved me from the enemy's grasp. Believing is simply not enough in a relationship. Wishing your marriage is going to last is not enough; work must be done. Hoping that something works out won't guarantee that it will, work must be done.

Most of us have heard James 2:26 being said in some way or fashion, simply put faith without works is dead. For me, that was my journey with God; you see, I always believed in God. There was never a time where I was an atheist; it just was not possible. I often tell people when God molded me in my mother's womb. He added a bunch of mustard seeds because He knew I was going to be a stubborn one.

I vividly remember since I was a child having this connection with the cross. I did not understand it, didn't know what it was about; I just had the strong urge to be near it. I remember when I was very young, I was having trouble sleeping, and my father thought it would be a good idea for us to go into the town square in Carini, Sicily (where I am from) and partake in the "walk to calvary". The *walk* was an annual parade type event where the Catholic clergy of our town would hold up a massive crucifix and the town people would follow behind them. They would walk for hours up and down the village as to mimic Jesus's final walk before he was crucified.

My dad thought I would get tired quickly, and then we could go home, and I could sleep. Well, the joke was on him. I remember clear as yesterday that I pushed people out of my way, because I NEEDED to be near Jesus on the cross. I made my way up to the cross near the clergymen. I got as close to the cross as possible. I also walked pretty much the entire walk until my dad picked me up and forced me home because he was exhausted.

Through my life journey, I realized that being catholic was not the right way, and so I later adapted the term Christian without really knowing what that meant. I ended up finding my first church home and went there when I could. During this time, I was going to the church house, and I was still super insecure, my addiction was out of control, I gave up custody of my son, I stole, I cheated, I loved drama and gossip was my favorite thing. Every other word was a cuss word, and I was a dreadful human being, BUT I went to the church house, and I believed in God.

One Sunday morning, the pastor did his typical altar call to salvation, I'm sure you know the one, it goes something like "if you were to die tonight and you are not sure where you would go then I urge you to invite Jesus into your heart and accept Him as your Lord and Savior. Join me in this prayer".

When he said that, I felt a little twinge in my spirit and realized that I was not sure where I would go. Alas, I didn't say that prayer or raised my hand, instead a week later while volunteering with a local ministry, I asked the Pastor Billy Hardwick (who I call OG) "how do you know that you are saved and going to heaven?" OG began to share the Gospel with me, not a prayer, but the Gospel and his testimony.

He began to share with me not just the love of Christ but about repentance and what that means, about what picking up your cross and following HIM meant. He began to share with me some things God spoke to him while his beautiful wife, Heather, was in labor with their boys. I remember sitting on a chair across from OG, soaking up everything he said. He was saying things I had never really heard or understood before. At that moment, I realized that I went to the church house on Sundays, yet every day I was headed to hell.

I made the decision sometime after to truly be adopted into the royal family of Christianity now that I knew about the Gospel, salvation, and what it meant to accept Jesus as my Lord (first) and Savior. I remember walking into the church house, lifting my hands high and telling God, "I am here, I surrender, I am yours," and the tears began to flow. I cried so hard my body was shaking, I felt warm like I was being soaked in a warm liquid from head to toe. I even heard a crack, and I began to scratch where my heart is, on my chest. God literally cracked the stone around my heart. A week later, I was baptized making my confession of faith public to my loved ones, OG and his wife Heather came and joined in prayer.

Once I was dry, I went to the altar on my knees, there was no altar call, but I needed to lay at the altar. I got on my knees, closed my eyes, and said, "Lord, if you see fit, please make me your servant". I remember thinking, "I hope you realized what you just asked for," however,

I just knew that despite whatever came my way, this was the right decision. One of the women (who would later become a mentor) came up to me afterward and said, "I hope you know; now it is on."

I didn't understand what she said. However, I later became extremely acquainted with spiritual warfare. I was never the same after that week, slowly but surely conviction came, OG began to disciple me, a few women took it upon themselves as it is stated in Titus 2 to mentor me. One by one, those chains began to fall, the more I learned about who God was, the importance of Jesus and His sacrifice on the cross, and what my role was in all of it, the more I was being set free.

The chains of addiction were broken, the chains of homosexuality were broken, the chains of sexual immorality (having sex before marriage, being addicted to porn, hypersexual behaviors) were broken, I was not stealing anymore, or cheating on anything. I earned sole custody of my son and began to be a mom after I was saved. I began to realize that not all attention is proper attention. I wanted nothing to do with drama and gossiping and being the star of the show. A year later, I stopped cussing, I have maybe said ten cuss words since 2017, and I'm still not happy with that. Anytime I say an ugly word, I feel so grimy, and I automatically go to God about it. In Christ, I have victory! I thank Him all the time for OG, his wife Heather, and the other women God put into my life to teach me.

Several months after accepting Christ, he sent a beautiful soul named Deborah Marshall (I love to call her name, DE-BO-RAH!), she sat with me, and did a Bible study called Women of Action, written by our pastor and one of the women in our church. Mrs. Deborah went thought the verses with me, patiently answered all my twisted questions, shared some testimonies with me, and met me right where I was, in all my sins just like Jesus did. Later, I became a part of Mrs. Deborah's next mission, which was Celebrate Recovery. I love Mrs. Deborah very much; that is the power of Titus 2 in all its glory.

With all those chains broken (and still many to go), I continued with bible studies with OG, my Titus 2 women, and myself. I learned about prayer, fasting, and spending time with God. All of this helped me to connect in ways that were very personal to me. I learned that God loves me so much He even spoke of the purpose of the bible so I wouldn't be left guessing.

In 2 Timothy 3:16-17, Paul wrote, "All scripture is God-breathed and is useful for teaching, rebuking, correcting and training in righteousness, so that the servant of God may be thoroughly equipped for every good work."

I was battling with insecurities, body shaming, self-hate; therefore, I learned what God said about the things I was struggling with because His word is the most important word and standard.

You would not believe the shock I was in when I found out about God's definition of beauty. It has nothing to do with gym memberships, a certain number of curves, or lack of on your body. It has nothing to do with clothes, jewelry, or a specific hair or eye color. 1 Peter 3:3-4 says, "Your beauty should not come from outward adornments, such as elaborate hairstyles and wearing gold jewelry or fine clothes. Rather it should be that of your inner self, the unfading beauty of a gentle and quiet spirit, which is of great worth in God's sight."

This verse literally left me in awe and in conviction all at the same time. I realized that I was made to think that I was not beautiful because of my outward appearance when that is not even what is worthy to God. Society has put such great emphasis on beauty and self-worth being linked to physical appearance. I have learned through this journey, and my faith walk that there is a vast difference between finding someone physically attractive (lust based) and finding someone beautiful (love-based).

Until we can understand the difference between these two, we will always be stuck in this pattern of "I'm not beautiful unless I look like this" or "I'm not beautiful because so and so doesn't like me". Placing unrealistic expectations on us, our bodies, and each other is how the enemy keeps us in chaos and disbelief of God's word.

One of my favorite lessons that God taught in the bible is found in 1 Samuel, chapter 16. Samuel is looking to anoint the next King, and he goes to a home where there are several son's (I encourage you to read that entire chapter for context). Samuel sees a young man who he just knew was the right man for the job. He was tall, strong, and pleasing to the eyes, all the characteristics that society would deem worthy.

However, in verse 17, God reveals something important (like I can't stress enough how vital it is) verse 17 states, "But the Lord said to Samuel, "Do not consider his appearance or his height, for I have rejected him. The Lord does not look at the things people look at. People look at the outward appearance, but the Lord looks at the heart." WOW! There is it, plain and simple, people look at the outward appearance, BUT the Lord looks at the heart. A pure heart produces a gentle and humble spirit, which is what God loves and finds

77

beautiful. I realized that God didn't put a weight restriction on beauty. He didn't even say anything wrong about women with facial hair. He drove two specific points, how we act and our heart condition, that's it!

It was in those 2:00 am Bible studies with the Lord, that I came to the revelation of a lifetime (outside of the salvation of course). Everything I had been told, made to feel, and believed about myself, my body, and being beautiful… was a lie. Well played satan well played! However, now that I knew better, I must do better. The question that then followed was, how? Romans 8:37 says, "…in all these things we are more than conquerors through Him who loved us." I was reminded that with and in Christ, I can get through anything.

I began to pray daily and seek scriptures like the ones mentioned before. I wrote them in index cards and posted them in my home and car. I found verses like Psalm 139:14. I carried Proverbs 3:5-6 everywhere I went. Reading and praying scriptures over and over every day. One day I even discovered a new way to read and apply scripture. A friend of mine sent me a link to a site that was transitioning out. They had beautiful rustic bracelets and necklaces with affirmation and scripture on them. I bought several pieces and then later became friends with the owner. I wore those pieces when I was having a bad self-esteem day. Anytime I wanted to walk with my head down, I read those messages, and I would spring back up. I had to get uncomfortable to grow out of the lies of the devil and walk upright into the truth of God.

I was at the doctor's office one morning; my stomach was bloated, my hair a mess, and my mustache decided to make an appearance. I felt horrible about myself, and then I looked down at the bracelet I had bought from that shop. It was a metal bracelet with Proverbs 3:15a engraved on it "She is more precious than rubies." I read it repeatedly until the doctor called my name. I stood up with my head held high and walked towards the door. *I am* worth more than rubies. God loved me so much that Jesus died on the cross for me! I and that includes my overweight body, my mustache and beard, my curly hair, my glasses, and everything I come with!

Later, my friend, who had that shop, moved into a new direction, and God led me to join her. Today, I have a small business called Anchored In Faith birthed out of Hebrews 6:19, where I sell everyday items, that speak life to women and young girls. I have done several outreaches with my business because I want everyone to know the truth.

Do I have bad days sometimes? Yes. Do I always feel my best? No. However, today I know what to do when those lies try to come at me. I know who to go to. I know what to speak over myself and who to believe. The word fat no longer means I am unworthy. My facial hair no longer means ugly. I can be called fat and KNOW that it means I am overweight, and it has nothing to do with my beauty. I can talk about my facial hair and know that I am loved.

One of my close friends even said to me two weeks ago, as we got into a conversation about body hair and our bodies in general, she said, "I love you and all of your hair." My friend Kelly Henry Smith told me one day when I talked severely about my face because of my facial hair "you better stop talking like that, that is God's hair." She is right, and therefore it's so important to be surrounded by people who love me and correct me because I am not perfect. I am also not even remotely as insecure as I used to be.

I started to wear dresses two years ago, which I would never have done before because of my weight. I began to wear different colors instead of all black all the time. My personality started to flourish because of God walking with me, teaching me His word, and meditating on it and keeping it with me and praying it daily.

One of my victories came on August 27, 2019, when I was planning on going to a recovery meeting. I was running late because laundry never ends. I rush my son into getting ready so that we could leave. I went to the bathroom to change, and I looked in the mirror. I could see my facial hair clear as day, my beard, mustache, all of it, and it wasn't even shaving day yet. I wanted to keep my hair up in a ponytail because it was so hot, and the humidity in the south is just straight disrespectful.

I had a choice to make; I could either run even later to the meeting and style my hair down so I could use it as curtains to cover my face or I could believe God's word and keep it in a ponytail and move on. I looked to the right of my mirror, where I had a large wooden sign with 1 Peter 3:3-4 on it, and I read it, took a deep breath, and kept my ponytail. I went to the meeting, shared, hung out with friends afterwards, forgot about my facial hair, and had a great and encouraging night. The world did not end because I had facial hair, my tribe didn't love me any less, and God reminded me of His beauty definition. The enemy, society, and my past cannot convince me to believe the lies anymore because I know the one who has conquered the world.

I know the one whose blood covers all sins. I am victorious because of my savior. My God made me with facial hair, my God sees my weight and health issues attached to that, and that same God made me more than a conqueror over my addiction.

Remember James 2:26, the infamous faith without works is dead verse? Two verses before that verse 24 states this "You see that a person is considered righteous by what they do and not by faith alone." My question to you is this: are you willing to accept the call to action, to get through and be in breakthrough, free from the bondage of insecurities?

CHAPTER 5

Call to Action

I have shared with you my journey; I have shared with you God's truth, and I have shared with you the warfare that comes and is. Now what? Time to fight back!

Before a battle or war soldiers put on their battle gear and grab their weapons. The first step to your call to action is exactly that, put on the armor. Now you might be saying, "umm what are you talking about?" I am glad you asked (again even if you did not).

The armor of God is a huge part of how to take action during spiritual warfare and moving forward to healing, revelation and the life God has destined you to live. Ephesians chapter 6:10-18 highlights why we need an armor and what it actually is. Starting with verse 10 "Finally, be strong in the Lord and in His mighty power." PAUSE, right off the bat, be strong in who? Your family? Friends? Partner/Spouse? Social media posts? Nope, be strong in the Lord and HIS mighty power, not the power of this new culture we got going on or society and its rules and popularity. Always keeping the foundation of you, built on God will guarantee everlasting freedom. Remember God is for you, He cannot lie, and He flows in love, mercy, and grace.

Verse 11, "Put on the full armor of God, so that you can take your stand against the devil's schemes." You see how the call is to put on the FULL armor, not just one piece? That is important to keep in mind. As well this verse told you why we need to (yes, we, I am not exempt from this either). "So that you can take your stand against the devil's schemes. This is how we take our stand, our position." Verse 12 "For our struggle is not against flesh and blood, but against the rulers, against the authorities, against the powers of this dark world and against the spiritual forces of evil in the heavenly realms."

HOLD UP! PAUSE! STOP! REWIND! Am I the only one that just caught that? Let's go back and analyze verse 12, "For our struggle is not against flesh and blood". So, you mean to tell me my struggles are not with my parents who planted seeds of self-hate with my weight? Nope. So, my struggles were not with the classmates that teased me about being a big girl? No. Okay so you mean to tell me my struggles aren't even with my own opinions of my facial hair? Not even close.

The struggle is between the spiritual forces of evil, the real battle is not with the people whom at face value seemed to have caused the hurt, it's via the *enemy himself.* Our adversary, the devil! Why is this so huge to understand? Because this gives us insight to spiritual reality, and this can also be the beginning of not only our healing ourselves but also forgiveness to those who have been used by the evil forces to hurt us. This is something the enemy does not want to happen: forgiveness. After all what better way to bring God honor then to forgive those who trespassed against us.

Now verse 13, "Therefore put on the full armor of God, so that when the day of evil comes, you may be able to stand your ground, and after you have done everything, to stand." It seems crucial that we are aware to put on the FULL armor, and why we need to do it since this is the second time it's been mentioned.

Verse 14 "Stand firm then, with the belt of truth buckled around your waist, with the breastplate of righteousness in place," that is the first piece of the armor, the belt of truth. What is the purpose of a belt? It holds things up right. Pants, tools, it can even be used to stop bleeding. Wrap yourself up with the truth, which is the word/ways of God. Satan speaks in lies; we stand firm with the truth.

The second piece mentioned is the breastplate of righteousness. The breastplate was used to protect the heart during war. Why should we protect our heart? Because pretty much all of us, in one way or another have reacted and have made bad decisions because of our emotions. We have all heard the saying "the heart wants what it wants" right? Usually this is said when it involves a bad or toxic person/relationship. Because the enemy attacks via feelings, we need to protect our hearts in righteousness.

Walk in the truth, give your heart condition to Christ, and protect yourself with the breastplate of righteousness. Remember feelings are not facts! Verse 15, "and with your feet fitted with the readiness that comes from the gospel of peace. When in action you always must be ready," and this means be ready to not only speak the truth over yourself but to others as well.

What is one of the reasons the enemy likes to keep us stuck in our insecurities? So, we don't share the Gospel. Part of the armor is the readiness to always be prepared to share it. Verse 16, "In addition to all this, take up the shield of faith, with which you can extinguish all the flaming arrows of the devil." The enemy will attack, with lies, through people, with life on life's terms, that is why we need the shield of faith which is walking in faith so we cannot be shaken as we stand firm.

When someone looks at me funny because I am walking around with facial hair, I walk in faith that I know who and whose I am and that my worth does not come from my appearance. Verse 17, "Take the helmet of salvation and the sword of the spirit, which is the word of God."

Two more parts of the armor, the helmet of salvation and the sword of the spirit. Why do people wear helmets? To protect their head. The helmet of salvation is there to protect your mind. However, take heart that salvation is a part of the armor as well, without salvation none of this can stand. The enemy is good at planting seeds of negativity, right? (how many times was this tactic mentioned in the book so far). However, if you are saved in Christ Jesus, and going through the process of sanctification then your mind is able to be protected because you have access to a relationship with God.

The other piece is the sword of the spirit and in that verse, we were also told what it was specifically and that is the word of God. A sword is a weapon, so how do we fight against the evil forces? With the word of God, we saw such a powerful example of how Jesus did that back in Chapter 3 when I highlighted Matthew 4. How do you defeat a lie? You attack it with the truth.

Whatever your insecurities are (and they can very well be different from mine), when the enemy calls you unworthy, you strike him with the sword of the spirit and repeat John 3:16. Finally verse 18, "and pray in the spirit on all occasions with all kinds of prayers and requests. With this in mind, be alert and always keep on praying for all the Lord's people". The final piece of the armor is prayer more specifically in the spirit.

Soldiers are trained to battle with a specific mindset. Nothing else matters, you move forward with the attitude of no matter how big the enemy is, it must be defeated. Also, during war, strategies and battle plans get put together and communicated with the officers. Praying in the spirit is our mindset and strategy session. God is the best commanding officer we got. One of the things I do to welcome in the spirit of God when I need to pray in the spirit is, I listen to specific worship songs. This helps me get into the mindset that nothing else matters right now, I need to seek guidance of my leader, my Lord, my God.

The second step is to put this armor on daily! Not just when you are having a bad day. Put it on when things are good, put it on when you are busy. Just put it on because 1 Peter 5:8b says "Your enemy the devil prowls around like a roaring lion looking for someone to devour." The enemy does not stop his evil plans, we should never stop putting on our armor. This way you know what to do when the enemy tries to talk you out of who God has called you to be. There is a need to saturate ourselves in God, like Samuel saturated David with the oil.

The third step to this call to action is find your village, your tribe, your community of believers. An army is not made up of one man, and even demons tend to operate in legions (Mark 5). Insecurities are contagious, and we all know misery loves company so being together with others that are going through the same thing as you or have experienced and have victories over the struggles you currently face is so important. Therefore, God is walking me through the process of building a mastermind class as I am writing this book. Not only to walk in my purpose to teach Gods word and show women how-to walk-in victory of their insecurities, but also to build an army of women where we fellowship together, pray for one another, and hold each other accountable.

You know how in movies before there is a battle scene there is a war cry? Or a sound being made from a trumpet or horn? Some tribes even have war dances. It signifies the beginning of the battle, a literal call to physical action. Here is your call!

Are you willing and ready to stand firm, put on your armor of God daily, and join an army of fellow warrior princesses? Are you ready and willing to walk in who God has called you to be?

I love how God does that, He never calls us by our past, mistakes, lies we believed or anything else but who we are destined to be. I love the fact that God did not choose Moses for a mission because of who Moses was, He chose Moses because of who He (God) knows himself to be. Another one of my favorites is Gideon (Lord knows I can be like Gideon). The angel of the Lord addressed Gideon as a mighty warrior even though at that moment Gideon was scared and in hiding.

Do *not* let the enemy continue to keep you bound by your insecurities. That is not the life God has for you, and that is not what I would want for you either. The enemy will use what you think about you and your current circumstance to keep you imprisoned so you do not fulfil the will of God. The devil is banking on you falling for the lies, versus falling on your knees in prayer. The adversary is hoping you will adapt the "live your truth" lifestyle instead of walking in the only truth that is Holy, the word of God. The tempter will continue to come at you, with temptations dressed up as feelings and desires in hopes that you follow your own heart versus following Jesus. There is a difference in knowing someone and knowing of someone, the same can be said for God and His word.

Through accepting this call to action, healing will come, forgiveness will flow and a deeper relationship with God will be built.

Before I ask one final question, I wanted to share with you one last personal testimony. On the day that this chapter was due to be sent to my editor, I struggled. In fact, I struggled all weekend long with health issues. Monday came around and as the deadline got closer and closer, I felt more fatigued, unfocused, and was in physical pain. I wanted to sleep, instead I remembered how we fight battles. I went into my room, I played worship music on repeat, and I praised and worshipped the Father. My pain started to lift; my fatigue started to vanish. It became even more clear to me that I was being attacked by the enemy so I wouldn't finish in time. I suited up and prayed. Within 40 minutes I was on my laptop with a focus I have not had in a while, and no physical pain. I was ready to write and turn in this last chapter, satan came, and he was defeated.

My story started with a prison, composed of concrete walls of insecurities (weight, facial hair, addiction). Each prison bar carved out of the stories that I have shared. The humiliation that came with crawling through the snow outside the bar to get one more fix. The heartbreak that came with my son rejecting my present. The embarrassment of that dreaded school desk. And just like the bars on the windows of the cell, somedays sunlight shines through them, bringing warmth and hope for a brighter day.

My sun rays were made of the hope shared in other stories, such as a text from a fellow sister, when I was engulfed in my selfishness of "wishing I had your problems" and the metal bracelet that reminded me I was worth more than rubies when I didn't feel like it. Rubies are valuable, just like I am, and thinking of jewels makes me think of royalty. I am royalty because my Abba (Father) is a king.

That dangerous, cold, hopeless prison, the small, lonely, and dark cell, the lies that I fully believed in, is no longer where I serve my time. That is no longer where I live, and that is no longer the mindset I operate in. I picked up my cross and followed HIM. I chose to follow God right out of that prison. I am now no longer an inmate of the enemy; I am now Abba's Little Princess.

The final question: are you willing to say enough is enough, step out of your prison, and accept the call to be Abba's Little Princess?

Abba's Little Princess